THE MYSTERY OF
ATLANTIS

Holly Wallace

Heinemann Library
Chicago, Illinois

© 1999, 2006 Heinemann Library
a division of Reed Elsevier Inc.
Chicago, Illinois

Customer Service 888-454-2279
Visit our website at www.heinemannraintree.com

Designed by Victoria Bevan and Q2A
Printed and bound in China by WKT

10 09 08 07 06
10 9 8 7 6 5 4 3 2 1

New edition ISBNs: 1-40348-331-0 (hardcover)
                   1-40348-340-X (paperback)

The Library of Congress has cataloged the hardcover editions as follows:
Wallace, Holly.
         The mystery of the Atlantis / Holly Wallace.
p. cm.—(Can science solve?)
Includes bibliographical references.
Summary: Examines the legend of the lost civilization of Atlantis and various
theories that seek to explain it.
         ISBN 1-57572-803-6 (lib. bdg.)   ISBN 1-58810-307-2 (pbk. bdg)
1. Atlantis—Juvenile literature. [1. Atlantis.]   I. Title.
II. Series
GN751.W35   1999
001.94.—dc21
                                                      99-54490
                                                         CIP
                                                         AC

Acknowledgments
The author and publishers are grateful to the following for permission to
reproduce copyright material:
Ancient Art and Architecture Collection: p. 11, R Sheridan pp. 8, 18, 19, G Tortoli
pp. 16, 20; Fortean Picture Library: pp. 7, 10, K Aarsleff p. 13, J and C Bord p. 22,
W Donato pp. 25, 27, Llewellyn Publications p. 24; Ronald Grant Collection: p. 5;
Oxford Scientific Films: R Packwood p. 14; Science Photo Library: p. 6, D Parker
p. 12; Still Pictures: C Guarita p. 28.

Cover photograph of sand sculptures, Belgium, reproduced with permission of
Empics/PA Photos/Reporters.

Every effort has been made to contact copyright holders of any material
reproduced in this book. Any omissions will be rectified in subsequent printings
if notice is given to the publisher.

The paper used to print this book comes from sustainable sources.

Some words are shown in bold, **like this**. You can find the definitions for these
words in the glossary.

CONTENTS

UNSOLVED MYSTERIES

For hundreds of years, people have been interested in and puzzled by mysterious places, creatures, and events. Is there really a monster living in Loch Ness, in Scotland? Are UFOs tricks of the light or actually vehicles from outer space? Who is responsible for mysterious crop circle patterns—clever fakers or alien beings? Did the lost land of Atlantis ever exist? Some of these mysteries have baffled scientists, who have spent years trying to find the answer. But just how far can science go? Are there some mysteries that science simply cannot solve? Read on, and make up your own mind . . .

In this book, you will learn about the lost land of Atlantis. Ever since the Greek writer Plato described Atlantis in the 4th century B.C., there have been theories about the city and what happened to it. This book also examines a range of theories about the city, dating from the 1880s right up to the 21st century. Read all the theories and then decide for yourself. Which one do you think is the most convincing?

What was Atlantis?

According to **legend**, Atlantis was an ancient island **civilization** in the Atlantic Ocean that existed about 12,000 years ago. Then, in the space of a night and a day, it sank without a trace beneath the waves. It was a powerful kingdom whose army had conquered large parts of Africa and Europe, before being defeated by the ancient Greeks. Its people enjoyed a **privileged** lifestyle, surrounded by fine things and beautiful palaces—until one fateful day, when their golden world came crashing down around them.

But did Atlantis ever actually exist? We have no eyewitness reports to go by. No ruins have ever been found. Apart from one ancient account, later theories have often been based more in science fiction than in scientific fact. And if Atlantis did exist, two questions still remain: where was it located and how was it finally destroyed? Was it a natural disaster or an act of the gods? Is there anything science can do to solve one of the greatest mysteries of all time?

Many books and movies have been based on the story of Atlantis, including this one, entitled *The Lost Kingdom*. This is a scene inside the fabulous royal palace of the Atlantean king.

BEGINNINGS OF A MYSTERY

The first and only sources we have for the mystery of Atlantis are two ancient accounts, both written by the Greek **philosopher** Plato in the 4th century B.C.E. They are written as imaginary conversations that take place between the philosopher Socrates and three friends. The two accounts are called *Timaeus* and *Critias*, named after their main characters. Plato began to work on a third account, but he never completed it.

Plato, the Greek philosopher, lived from 428–347 B.C.E. The **legend** of Atlantis began with his ancient accounts. But were they historical fact or merely a story? No one knows.

Two accounts

In his version of events, Plato puts the story of Atlantis into the mouth of the poet and historian Critias. He says that he heard the story as a child from his grandfather, who had heard it from his own father. He, in turn, had heard it from his friend Solon (c. 640–558 B.C.E.), a famous Greek politician from Athens who had been told the story by an elderly Egyptian priest. By the priest's time, the story was already very old, recorded in the ancient temple records. It tells how, about 9,000 years before Solon's birth, or about 12,000 years ago, Atlantis was a rich, powerful island in the Atlantic Ocean whose armies conquered many of the lands around the Mediterranean, until they were finally defeated by the Athenians. This is Plato's account of the Egyptian priest's words:

"There was an island situated in front of the **straits** that you call the Pillars of Hercules [now called the Straits of Gibraltar] and that was larger than Libya and Asia Minor [modern Turkey] put together. . . . Now on this island of Atlantis there was a great and wonderful **empire** that ruled over the whole island and several others, and over parts of the **continent**, and controlled, within the straits, Libya as far as Egypt and Europe as far as Tyrrhenia [Italy]. This vast power attempted to **subdue** both my country [Egypt] and yours [Greece] and the whole region within the strait. Then, Solon, your country defeated the invaders and saved us all from slavery. But afterward, there occurred violent earthquakes and floods, and in a single day and night, the island of Atlantis was swallowed up by the sea and disappeared."

This is a map of Atlantis from the 1644 book *Mundus Subterraneus* (The Underground World), by Dutch writer Athanasius Kircher. He based his guess at Atlantis's location on Plato's accounts.

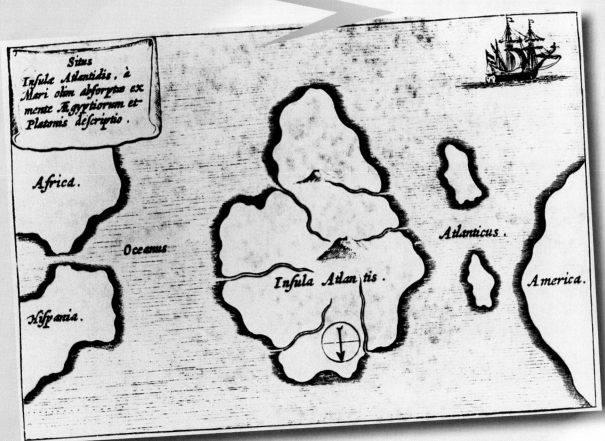

Situs
Insulæ Atlantidis, à
Mari olim abforptæ ex
mente Ægyptiorum et
Platonis defcriptio.

Africa.

Oceanus

Hyfpania.

Infula Atlantis.

Atlanticus.

America.

WHAT WAS ATLANTIS LIKE?

In his second account, *Critias*, Plato described the history, geography, and people of Atlantis in more detail. He tells how the kings of Atlantis were created by Poseidon, the ancient Greek god of earthquakes and the sea. They were great architects and engineers, building temples, palaces, and harbors. Their capital city was circular in shape and built on a hill, surrounded by alternate rings of land and water that were joined by huge bridges and tunnels. A huge canal connected the outermost ring of water to the sea. Behind the city was a great, fertile plain where farmers grew the city's food. The island was also rich in minerals, timber, and exotic animals, including elephants.

According to **legend**, the people of Atlantis were descended from the sea god, Poseidon. Atlantis took its name from the giant Atlas, one of Poseidon's sons.

This is an artist's impression of the gardens of the magnificent palace of the king of Atlantis. But did it really exist?

A magnificent palace

According to Plato, the priest told Solon how the king of Atlantis lived in a luxurious palace on top of the hill. In the center of the palace stood a temple to Poseidon. This is how Plato describes it:

"The outside of the temple was covered in silver, apart from the **pinnacles**. The pinnacles were covered in gold. Inside, the roof was made of ivory, decorated with gold, silver, and other precious metals. All the other walls and pillars were lined with precious metals. In the temple they placed golden statues—there was Poseidon himself standing in a chariot pulled by six winged horses, and of such a size that he touched the roof of the temple with his head."

It seemed the Atlanteans had everything they could wish for. But, says Plato, they became greedy and corrupt (immoral). Zeus, the king of the gods, decided to teach them a lesson and destroyed their golden land as punishment.

However, even 50 years after Plato's death, doubts began over whether his Atlantis was a real place. Had the story truly been passed down to him as he claimed, or had he invented it in order to discuss the politics of his own city, Athens? Was the account historical fact or just a story? The debate continues today.

9

INTEREST RENEWED

Modern interest in Atlantis began in the 19th century with the publication, in 1882, of an extraordinary book called _Atlantis: the Antediluvian World_. Written by a U.S. politician, Ignatius Donnelly, the book quickly became a best-seller all over the world. The cult of Atlantis was born.

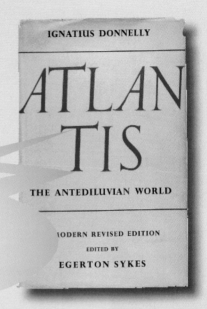

This is the cover of Donnelly's best-selling book, _Atlantis: the Antediluvian World_. It sparked off a huge amount of interest in the mystery of Atlantis.

Donnelly's theory

Donnelly firmly believed that Atlantis had existed and that it had ended exactly as Plato described. He placed the island in the Azores in the mid-Atlantic (see page 16) and made the following claims to back up his theory:

- A large island, Atlantis, once existed in the Atlantic Ocean. It was all that remained of an Atlantic **continent**.

- Plato's description was historical fact.

- **Civilization** itself began in Atlantis.

- Atlantis was a mighty power that conquered many other countries.

- It was the true antediluvian world.

- The oldest colony founded by the Atlanteans was in Egypt.

- The Atlanteans were the first people to use iron and bronze.

- The Atlanteans invented the first alphabet.

- Atlantis was destroyed by a natural disaster, such as an earthquake or volcanic eruption.

- A few people escaped on rafts and ships.

A lack of evidence

Donnelly based his theories on his reading of Plato's account of Atlantis and on his own study of a variety of sciences, including **zoology** and **geology**. In the 19th century, these "new sciences" were beginning to be studied and taken seriously for the first time. His claims captured the imagination of a great many people, but serious scientists dismissed them as nonsense. After all, there was no hard evidence whatsoever to back them up.

Sun worship

From his study of ancient religions, Donnelly concluded that the people of Atlantis worshipped the Sun and that their religion spread to ancient Egypt and Peru. Since then, **archaeologists** have discovered many Egyptian paintings showing worship of the Sun god, Ra, and mysterious carvings of the Sun in the Nazca desert in Peru. Could Donnelly's claims be true?

This Egyptian painting shows the Sun god, Ra, traveling in his "solar barge" between Nut, the sky goddess (above), and Geb, the Earth god (below).

OTHER THEORIES

Although many people dismissed Donnelly's book as pure speculation, it sparked off a huge amount of interest in Atlantis. Thousands of books, articles, and short stories followed, and the name of Atlantis was used on everything from ships to a region of the planet Mars. There were hundreds of other theories, too, some based, if loosely, in science, and others that were completely made up. Here are just some of them . . .

This huge crater in Arizona was formed when a giant meteorite hit Earth about 50,000 years ago. Could an even larger meteorite have caused Atlantis to sink?

Bombardment from space

Several theories suggest that Atlantis was destroyed by an enormous **meteorite** hitting Earth. In 1976 German scientist and engineer Otto Muck published his book *The Secret of Atlantis*. In it he points to two huge depressions (holes), 4.3 miles (7 kilometers) deep on the sea floor in the western Atlantic, as likely **impact craters**. Scientifically, this could have been possible—in 1920 a meteorite weighing 65 tons (59 tonnes) struck Namibia in Africa, the largest meteorite yet known. But Muck calculates that the Atlantic meteorite must have been 6.2 miles (10 kilometers) wide and claims that it also split the Atlantic Ocean open along the line of the Mid-Atlantic Ridge, a long chain of underwater mountains running down the middle of the Atlantic Ocean. Science has since proved this to be untrue (see pages 16–17).

Evidence from eels

In his book, Muck also suggested that the sinking of Atlantis could explain the mysterious **migrations** of eels across the Atlantic. Each year, European eels leave their river homes and swim across the Atlantic to the Sargasso Sea to breed. Then, the tiny **elvers** begin an incredible 3,700-mile (6,000-kilometer), three-year-long journey home, carried on the warm waters of the Gulf Stream current. Muck wondered why the eels would risk such a long and dangerous journey. He suggested that the Gulf Stream once circled Atlantis and carried the eels to fresh water by a much shorter, more direct route. When Atlantis sank, it broke the flow of the Gulf Stream and made the eels' journey much longer.

Pyramid parallels

Some people, including Lewis Spence, a writer from Scotland, tried to link Atlantis to the **civilizations** of Central and South America. Between the 1920s and the 1940s, he wrote several books pointing to similarities between, for example, the pyramids built by the Mayas in Mexico and those built by the ancient Egyptians, whose country was supposedly ruled by Atlantis. However, many historians do not believe that the two are linked.

This is a Mayan pyramid in Mexico. Because it was similar in shape to the pyramids of ancient Egypt, supposedly a colony of Atlantis, Spence suggested that its building may have been influenced by Atlantean culture.

ATLANTIS FOUND?

So, if Atlantis did exist, where was it located? According to Plato, "It was an island situated in front of the **straits** that are called the Pillars of Hercules." This places it to the west of the Straits of Gibraltar (called the Pillars of Hercules by the Greeks) in the Atlantic Ocean. But not everyone agrees. Some of the other locations suggested for Atlantis include the United States, Scandinavia, the Canary Islands, and even Greenland. You can read more about possible locations on the following pages.

Spanish lands

In 2004 Dr. Rainer Kuehne suggested that the lost "island" of Atlantis was once a large region off the southwest coast of Spain. This sunken area was flooded by a **tsunami** around 12,000 years ago. This is roughly the same time as the earthquake and floods that Plato described swallowing up Atlantis. The sunken Spanish lands lie close to the Straits of Gibraltar—exactly where Plato said Atlantis could be found. However, these lands were originally part of Spain, while Plato wrote about an island.

This is the summit (top) of the Rock of Gibraltar. In ancient times, this rock and Mount Hacho, in modern Morocco, were known as the Pillars of Hercules, marking the division between the Mediterranean Sea and the Atlantic Ocean.

Satellite evidence?

In 2005 pictures taken by a satellite camera showed the ocean bed off the southwest coast of Spain. These pictures may support Dr. Kuehne's theory that Atlantis was once part of Spain. The satellite pictures appear to show some large, rectangular buildings and some tall walls. Could these be the ruins of the great city described by Plato?

Northern Europe

In his 1976 book, *Atlantis of the North*, German scholar Dr. Jürgen Spanuth tried to prove that Atlantis was located off the northwest coast of Germany, where there was a group of sunken islands. He also claimed that the people of Atlantis were, in fact, the early ancestors of the Vikings. However, no evidence has yet been found to support his claim.

Antarctic Atlantis

U.S. author Alan F. Alford suggested in his 1996 book, *Gods of the New Millennium*, that Atlantis may have been situated in Antarctica. He says that, at the time given by Plato for Atlantis's existence, which was about 12,000 years ago, Antarctica was ice free. When the region did freeze over, which was about 6,000 years ago, according to Alford, its people (the Atlanteans) spread far and wide throughout the world, including Egypt, where they built the pyramids. It is true that Antarctica was not always a frozen **continent**. It once had a much warmer climate than today. But from the **geological** study of ancient rock and ice samples, scientists know that Antarctica was largely covered in ice two to three million years ago, so Alford's theory could not be correct.

EARTH MOVEMENTS

In his book (see page 10), Ignatius Donnelly suggested that the likeliest site for Atlantis was the Azores, a group of islands in the middle of the North Atlantic. This theory has now been disproved by geologists.

This is an island in the Azores, where Donnelly believed Atlantis to lie. Since then, his theory has been proved to be scientifically impossible.

Earth's crust

Earth's hard, outer crust is not one single layer of rock. It is split into seven huge and numerous smaller pieces called plates. The plates are constantly floating, or drifting, on the layer of red-hot, liquid rock, or magma, lying beneath them. This is called continental drift. Usually this happens without anyone noticing. Sometimes, though, the plates collide or pull apart violently, causing earthquakes and volcanoes.

Mid-Atlantic Ridge

In the middle of the Atlantic Ocean, two plates of crust are slowly pulling apart. Over millions of years, magma has welled up to plug the gap, then hardened and been pushed upward to form a chain of mountains. This process is called sea-floor spreading. The chain of mountains is the Mid-Atlantic Ridge, the longest mountain range on Earth. It runs down the entire length of the Atlantic, splitting it in two and rising to the surface in only a few places, including the Azores.

Disproving Donnelly

Donnelly claimed that the Azores were the mountaintops of a large, sunken island, namely Atlantis. By the time that Donnelly's book came out (1882), the Mid-Atlantic Ridge had been discovered, but very little was known about its **geology**. The modern science of **oceanography** (the study of the oceans) has shown that the Azores are, in fact, islands that have grown up from the seabed as a result of sea-floor spreading. They cannot be Atlantis.

Continental drift

The first person to claim that the crustal plates moved was a German scientist, Alfred Wegener, in 1915. He suggested that, about 200 million years ago, all the land was joined together as one huge continent, called Pangaea. It was surrounded by a vast ocean, Panthalassa. Over millions of years, the plates drifted apart and Pangaea split up, eventually forming the continents and oceans we have today. Until the 1960s, Wegener's theory was not taken seriously. Then, geologists discovered that the plates did indeed move. They also found fossil evidence of plants and dinosaurs to support the idea that the continents were once linked, as Wegener said.

Panthalassa · Pangaea · Panthalassa

200 million years ago

Pacific-Ocean · Atlantic Ocean · Southern Ocean · Pacific-Ocean · Indian-Ocean

65 million years ago

Present day

Key
——— plate boundaries

North American plate

Eurasianplate

Caribbeanplate

Chinaplate

Pacificplate

Philippineplate

Africanplate

LOOKING AT THE PAST

One of the most believable theories about the location of Atlantis places it in the Mediterranean Sea, on the Greek island of Crete. It was here, about 4,000 years ago, that a mighty civilization grew up that had many similarities with Plato's Atlantis. Could they be one and the same? Some scientists think they might be.

Rediscovering the Minoans

Our knowledge of the Minoans, the people who lived on Crete some 4,000 years ago, comes from archaeological evidence found on Crete. In 1900 British **archaeologist** Sir Arthur Evans began **excavating** the magnificent royal palace at Knossos. He uncovered a civilization far more advanced and sophisticated than anything yet found in Europe. Evans called it Minoan, after a **legendary** ruler named King Minos.

This is part of the ruined Minoan palace of Knossos. Some scientists believe that the Atlanteans and Minoans may have been one and the same people.

Similarities . . .

From Evans's discoveries (see above), other scholars drew similarities between Minoan and Atlantean culture. The Minoans built their towns around magnificent royal palaces. The largest and grandest was at Knossos. Did Plato hear about this and base his description of the royal palace in Atlantis on it? Or had the story reached the ancient Egyptians, who had passed it to Solon as Plato claimed (see pages 6–9)?

This is a **fresco** from Knossos showing the ancient sport of bull-leaping. Both the Atlanteans and Minoans were said to have worshipped bulls as sacred animals.

Evans also found many paintings and sculptures of bulls, which were sacred (holy) animals for the Minoans. Plato described a similar **cult** of bull-worship on Atlantis.

Finally, both the Minoans and Atlanteans met a mysterious and violent end. In about 1500 B.C.E., Minoan civilization was destroyed by a series of natural disasters, including earthquakes and tidal waves—similar to the "violent earthquakes and floods" that Plato said destroyed Atlantis . . .

. . . and differences

So, could Crete be Atlantis? Despite the similarities, there are problems with the theory. First, Crete was not a round island, as Plato described Atlantis to be, and it did not sink beneath the sea and vanish without a trace. Second, it is not located in the Atlantic. However, Minoan script (writing), called Linear A, found on clay tablets and discs from Crete, is not yet fully understood by archaeologists. Who knows what secrets it might hold . . .

A VIOLENT VOLCANO

Many experts have linked the collapse of Minoan civilization to the violent eruption of Thera, a volcanic island about 68.4 miles (110 kilometers) to the north of Crete. Or could Thera itself have been Atlantis?

Excavations at Akrotiri on Santorini (Thera) have uncovered a great city in Minoan style. Could these be the long-lost ruins of Atlantis?

Thera erupts

The traditional date given for the eruption of Thera is 1450 B.C.E., about the same time as the Minoan collapse. So violent was the explosion that most of Thera was blown away, leaving only a small, crescent-shaped island that is now also called Santorini. This may have caused tidal waves, flooding, and earth tremors (vibrations) on Crete. Recent archaeological evidence suggests, however, that Thera may have erupted some 200 years earlier and may not have been responsible for the destruction of Minoan Crete. Even if these two dates matched, they still placed the destruction of Atlantis just 900 years before Solon, not 9,000, as Plato claimed.

Thera as Atlantis

So, could Thera have been the **catastrophe** that destroyed Atlantis?
Greek **archaeologist** Professor Spyridon Marinatos certainly thought
so. He also believed that Thera was linked to Crete, possibly as a result
of the spread of Minoan culture throughout the Mediterranean. In 1967
he began **excavating** at Akrotiri, in the southwest of Santorini (Thera).
Buried under layers of volcanic ash, Marinatos found the remains of a
great city, with streets of Minoan-style houses and **frescos** showing a
highly advanced civilization. As for the problem of dates, he suggested
a scribe (writer) had simply written the wrong dates down, multiplying
everything by ten.

Another possibility is that Thera itself was Atlantis. After all, scientists
know that, during the eruption that destroyed the island, the central
part of the island sank into the sea.

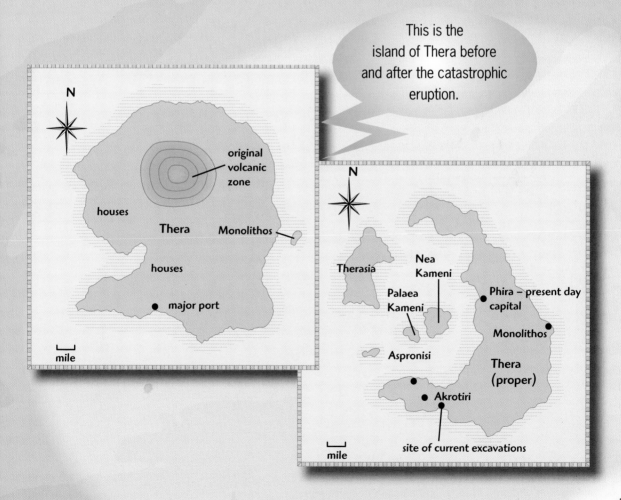

This is the island of Thera before and after the catastrophic eruption.

N

original volcanic zone

houses

Thera   Monolithos

houses

● major port

mile

N

Therasia

Nea Kameni

Palaea Kameni

Phira – present day capital

Monolithos

Aspronisi

Thera (proper)

● Akrotiri

site of current excavations

mile

OTHER SUNKEN CITIES

Atlantis-hunters have not given up hope of finding their lost land. After all, they argue, there are many other examples of ancient places that have been rediscovered, thousands of years after sinking beneath the sea. They include the ancient Greek port of Apollonia in Libya, which was built in about 630 B.C.E., and Port Royal, the pirate city described below. One day, the ruins of Atlantis may be among them.

Lost kingdom

A group of rocks called the Seven Sisters lies in the sea, about 6.2 miles (10 kilometers) off Land's End, the southernmost tip of Great Britain. According to **legend**, they mark the site of a kingdom that once linked Britain to France. It was called Lyonesse. In the fifth century C.E., a huge wave swept over Lyonesse and it disappeared beneath the sea. There was only one survivor. Since then, local fishermen have hauled up many fragments of buildings and other objects in their nets. They claim that these come from Lyonesse.

This is one of the Seven Sisters rocks off Land's End, in Cornwall, England. This was said to be the site of the lost kingdom of Lyonesse which, like Atlantis, sank into the sea.

Diving dilemmas

There are many problems with diving to look for ruins. As divers go deeper, the weight of the water pressing down on them increases. This weight is called water pressure. This produces bubbles of gas in their blood. If they surface too quickly, the bubbles cause a painful, sometimes deadly condition called the bends. To avoid this, divers spend time in a decompression chamber, where they slowly and safely return to normal pressure. Of course, some problems are more difficult to overcome than others. Take, for example, this theory of why divers have not yet found Atlantis—namely that, as they dive, they enter another dimension . . .

Port Royal

On June 7, 1692, the pirate harbor of Port Royal, Jamaica, slumped into the sea. Just before midday, the city was hit by a massive and disastrous earthquake. The whole of the waterfront, complete with streets, houses, and stores, slid into the sea. A huge tidal wave swept over the city and, in two short minutes, two-thirds of the city had been swallowed up and 2,000 people were dead. For hundreds of years, the ruins of Port Royal lay underwater. Then, in 1959, a U.S. ship, *Sea Diver*, specially equipped with **echo sounders** and **radar**, explored the site. Further **excavations** by divers and **archaeologists** followed in the 1960s. Thousands of **artifacts** were found.

STRANGE STORIES

As you have seen, there are many different theories about Atlantis. Some have been very carefully thought out, taking science and history into account to try to solve the mystery. Often, however, the science used has since been proved wrong. Other theories are much, much stranger, without any basis in science at all. Many have been put forward by people called occultists whose interest lies in the world of the supernatural.

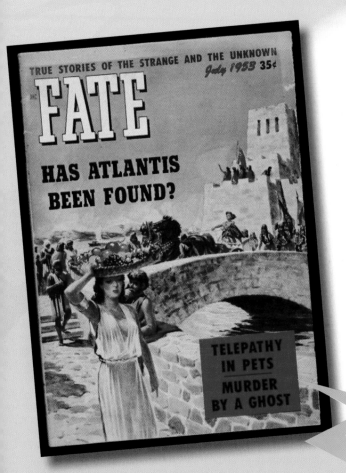

TRUE STORIES OF THE STRANGE AND THE UNKNOWN July 1953 35¢

FATE

HAS ATLANTIS BEEN FOUND?

TELEPATHY IN PETS

MURDER BY A GHOST

Atlantis rising

Atlantology is the name given to the study, scientific or otherwise, of Atlantis. Many Atlantologists believe that, one day, Atlantis will rise again. This may not mean that the island will physically rise from the sea, but that there will be a return of the qualities and virtues of goodness, courage, and wisdom that made Atlantis great. The only question is . . . when?

Although many theories have been disproved, the possibility of finding Atlantis still excites both **archaeologists** and those interested in the supernatural.

The fourth race

In 1877 Russian occultist Helena Blavatsky published a huge book called *Isis Unveiled*. It contained just one page on Atlantis. In it, Madame Blavatsky claimed that the people of Atlantis were the fourth "race" on Earth, a super-human people who lived long before the present human beings and who had amazing **psychic** powers. However, they were corrupted (made immoral) by a great dragon king, Thevetat, and turned into wicked magicians. They began a war that ended with Atlantis being submerged under water.

In her next book, *The Secret Doctrine*, published after she died, Madame Blavatsky had more to say. The book is a commentary on an ancient text said to have been actually written in Atlantis. Among her many claims, she tells how the survivors of Atlantis settled in Egypt and built the pyramids about 100,000 years ago. However, modern science shows that the earliest were actually built in about 2600 B.C.E.

Toltec ancestors

In the 1890s, another occultist, W. Scott-Elliott, claimed to be able to read the so-called "Akasic Records." These were a secret history of ancient wisdom, said to exist on the "astral plane," another dimension beyond normal life. From his reading, he claimed that Atlantis had existed an incredible one million years ago. There were seven races of Atlanteans, one of which was the Toltecs. In conventional history, the Toltecs were a nomadic (wandering) people of Mexico. They built their capital at Tula, north of Mexico City, in about C.E. 900.

This is a huge statue of a Toltec warrior.

A FALSE START

In the 1920s, a U.S. clairvoyant, Edgar Cayce, claimed that he had spent one of his past lives in Atlantis. According to him, Atlantis reached from the Sargasso Sea to the Azores and was about the size of Europe. Its land and civilization had been destroyed twice, in the course of which the mainland had been split into islands. The last to sink was near the Bahamas, off the coast of Florida. In 1940 Cayce predicted that this part of Atlantis would rise again, some time around 1968. But was he right?

Fakes and frauds

In the 1870s, German archaeologist Heinrich Schliemann discovered the ruins of the ancient city of Troy in Turkey, the site of the **legendary** Trojan War. Forty years later, his grandson, Paul, claimed that Troy and Atlantis had been allies (on the same side). He said that his grandfather had found a bowl at Troy inscribed with the words "From King Cronos of Atlantis." Archaeologists later proved that the bowl was a fake.

The Bimini Road

Early in 1968, an **archaeologist**, Dr. J. Manson Valentine, found a J-shaped pathway of rectangular stone slabs about 2,300 feet (700 meters) long and lying several feet under water off the coast of North Bimini, in the Bahamas. It became known as the Bimini Road. There was great excitement. Had Atlantis been found, as Cayce had predicted? One Atlantis-hunter had no doubt. He claimed that the stones were part of an ancient Atlantean temple. One of them might even be the head of a stone statue.

Scientists disagreed. Some said that the pavement had been formed naturally. Others accepted that it could be human-made but was likely to be the remains of a sea wall that had sunk beneath the water. In 1981, in the course of an **oceanographic** survey of the area, the U.S. **Geological** Survey solved at least part of the mystery by proving that the "Road" had indeed been laid down by natural means between 2,500 and 3,500 years ago—long after Atlantis.

This is a glimpse of the Bimini Road. You can just spot the J-shaped pathway of stones beneath the water.

WHAT DO YOU THINK?

So, can science help us find Atlantis? Unfortunately, the lack of solid and reliable evidence means that the answer is probably, "No—at least not at the moment." Remember that there are dozens of researchers who have studied the mystery of Atlantis closely, and yet still there is no definite proof. Did the island ever exist, and, if so, can it be found?

Could Crete be Atlantis?

Sounds convincing . . .
- The island of Crete was home to an ancient civilization—just like Plato's island of Atlantis.

- The Minoan people of Crete worshipped bulls —just like the Atlantean people.

- The Minoan civilization on Crete was destroyed by a series of disasters, including earthquakes and floods.

But what about . . . ?
- The fact that the island of Crete is in the Mediterranean Sea, not the Atlantic.

- The island of Crete never sunk beneath the sea.

- Crete is not a round island, like the one that Plato described.

This is the great city of Athens, Greece, as it appears today. Was Plato really talking about Athens, not Atlantis, in his famous accounts? If so, perhaps Atlantis only existed in his imagination.

Supporters of the theory that Crete was the lost island of Atlantis suggest that the mysterious Minoan script (writing) might hold the answer to the mystery.

What about the other theories about Atlantis? Do you think some of them might be true? Look at the list of theories below and decide which you think are the most convincing.

- Atlantis was the first ancient civilization. Its religion of sun worship spread to ancient Egypt and Peru.

- The most likely site for Atlantis was the Azores, a group of islands in the North Atlantic.

- Atlantis was originally a region on the southwest coast of Spain. This area was flooded by a **tsunami** around 12,000 years ago.

- The volcanic island of Thera was Atlantis. When Thera erupted in 2450 B.C.E., most of the city was destroyed.

- Atlantis can be found in Germany, Brazil, or the Antarctic.

Do you think any of these theories can be discussed without further investigation? Do you have any theories of your own? Perhaps one of the theories here is the answer, but it depends on scientific facts that we don't understand yet.

Try to keep an open mind. Remember that science is constantly developing, and new discoveries are being made all the time. Just because something can't be proved scientifically now, it doesn't mean this will always be the case.

GLOSSARY

antediluvian time before the flood. There are many myths about a great flood sent by the gods to punish people for becoming wicked. Before this, they lived for centuries in peace and happiness in paradise.

archaeologist scientist who studies the past by looking at ancient ruins and remains

artifact ancient object, such as a pot, a piece of jewelry, or a weapon, that helps to tell archaeologists about the past

catastrophe sudden, widespread disaster

civilization people and their society

clairvoyant person who claims to have the power to look into the future

continent large mass of land

cult religious group or a group devoted to an idea

echo sounder instrument used to measure the depth of the water and to map the features of the seabed. It gives out pulses of sound that hit parts of the sea floor and send back echoes. The pattern of the echoes is traced onto a screen to create a picture of the sea floor.

elver young eel

empire large group of countries ruled by one strong power

excavate to reveal something by digging away what covers it

fresco painting drawn on wet plaster

geology scientific study of the rocks of Earth's crust

impact crater deep hollow in the ground left when a meteorite hits Earth

legend story that may or may not be true

legendary based on a legend, which may or may not be true

meteorite lump of space rock that originally comes from comets and that sometimes crashes into Earth

migration long journey made by some fish, birds, and mammals between their feeding and breeding grounds

occultist person who is interested in the supernatural

oceanography study of the oceans. It is a mixture of different sciences—biology, geology, chemistry, physics, and meteorology.

philosopher person who studies the meaning behind life and the universe. In ancient Greece, philosophers were people who studied all aspects of the world around them.

pinnacle decorative tower on a roof

privileged lucky or honored

psychic person who claims to read people's minds and see into the future

radar instrument used to detect the direction, range, and presence of objects that show up on a screen

strait narrow channel connecting two large areas of water

subdue to put down

tsunami large wave caused by an earthquake under the sea or an underwater volcanic eruption

zoology scientific study of animals

Find Out More

You can find out more about the Atlantis in books and on the Internet. Use a search engine such as www.yahooligans.com to search for information. A search for the word "Atlantis" will bring back lots of results, but it may be difficult to find the information you want. Try narrowing your search to look for some of the people and ideas mentioned in this book, such as "Seven Sisters" or "Helena Blavatsky."

More Books to Read

Donkin, Andrew. *Atlantis: The Lost City?* New York: DK, 2000.

Townsend, John. *Out There? Mysteries of the Deep*. Chicago: Raintree, 2004.

INDEX